An Essential Guide to Minimalism

A minimalist guide to achieving more in life by having less

Table of Contents

About The Author 3
Book Description 4
Chapter 1: What you get from living a Minimalist Life 5
Chapter 2: Minimalism and the Search for Happiness 12
Chapter 3: Minimalism as Counter Consumerism 21
Chapter 4: Letting Go and Moving On 43
Chapter 5: Minimalism and Financial Freedom 54
Chapter 6: Minimalism and Decluttering 62
Conclusion 69

About The Author

George Pain is an entrepreneur, author and business consultant. He specializes in setting up online businesses from scratch, investment income strategies and global mobility solutions. He has built several businesses from the ground up, and is excited to share his knowledge with readers.

Book Description

This book guides you through the principles of Minimalism and why it is becoming a trend. It also guides you through the process of transformation to becoming a minimalist. The chapters show that minimalism is not just freeing yourself from material things but letting go of negative emotions, habits, attitude and perspective that bind you to the past and keep you from moving on. The book guides you to financial freedom where money no longer is the dominant force that drives you, but a means you can control in going after your goal of financial freedom.

Decluttering is also discussed but in a wider scope, touching on the benefits you get from decluttering and giving you tips on how to go about letting go of the clutter. Letting go and focusing on the essentials ultimately brings you the joy and contentment people search for. Whether you view Minimalism as a movement or a way of life, it frees you from life's present-day difficulties and gives hope of deliverance. It makes you look forward to a life where you are free to do what you want, have enough time to spend with people who matter to you, and grow as a person.

Chapter 1: What you get from living a Minimalist Life

In this chapter, I am going to tell you what you need to know about minimalism as a countermeasure against the stress of living. The chapter attempts to answer the following questions:

- What are the underlying reasons behind people who experience stress?
- What are the different perceptions of people on minimalism?
- What are the features that the concept of minimalism possesses?
- How does one become a minimalist?
- Is minimalism attainable?

It is easy to become frustrated living in a modern society. Life in modern-day society is full of physical, emotional, and mental tensions. Everything is in a rush with the time-clock dominating each day. Anywhere you turn, you face difficulties that threaten your relationship with coworkers, friends, and family members. Ultimately, you give up in fatigue and frustration.

A minimalist life could be the answer for you. But going minimalist without the full understanding of what minimalism in essence is and what you get from living a minimalist life can lead to frustrations. This chapter provides you with the weapon to prepare you for a minimalist way of life.

Modern-day culprits of a stressful life

Before things get even darker, look at the reasons for the frustrations to check out the bigger picture. Identifying common modern-day problems puts things in the right perspective and allow you to reflect and assess your situation.

- *Having a materialistic outlook.* It is in man's nature to pursue something for an unsatisfied need. The problem comes in when a need satisfied leads to wanting for more. Wanting for more than what you need, you find yourself cluttered with unnecessary things that occupy space, limiting your mobility.

For instance, buying figurines that catch your eye only to get lost on a shelf crowded with bric-a-brac. The beauty of the figurine which attracted you enough to make a purchase, but it suddenly loses its value when placed among the many others. You regret the purchase, and you feel guilty about it. Or, you add an outfit to a wardrobe that fills an already overflowing closet.

You do not need these purchases and only served to clutter your space. Studies would show you of a close link between your possessions and your physical and mental health. The findings show that people who base their happiness on material possessions tend to feel a decreased satisfaction in life.

- *Negativity.* Negativity in life only makes your life worse than it already is. Having negative values tends to multiply this, adding stress to your life. Negativity has the effect of making you lose your confidence and self-esteem; it robs you of happiness, joy, and depletes your energy.
- *Lack of self-control and discipline.* Your environment is full of distractions which pull you away from your goal in life. To counter the distraction in your environment, you need self-control and discipline to stay focused. Much of a person's behavior, however, started from childhood and developed throughout the adult stage. But, it is wrong to think that self-discipline is difficult to achieve and requires much sacrifice from you. Self-control is attainable, and if you stay focused on your goal, your chances of reaching your goal are higher.

Understanding Minimalism

There are many ways to define minimalism and differences in how people perceive minimalism. For some, minimalism is a way of life while for others it is a movement where everything - things, ideas, and space - pare down to the essentials in life. To understand what minimalism is, it helps to tackle some features minimalism possess.

1. *Priorities and Intentionality.* Minimalism is about evaluating your priorities in life and the will to deal with prioritized possessions, relationships, ideas, and activities. Anything not in your priorities should be discarded to avoid distractions. What you want and why you choose your priorities should be clear to you. It is when you are not clear with your needs that your will weakens. Before you know it, you are backsliding from a minimalist way of life to a life of possessing more.

2. *What matters are the essentials in life.* Most modern people grew up believing that happiness lies in possessions, that having more equates to happiness. The mania for possessions is a recent phenomenon influenced by elements like the media, advertisements that promote products, new products coming out in the market which are variations of the same product etc. A person inevitably gets pulled into

the world of consumerism, buying more than what is needed.

But, if you look back in human history, the early people – the nomads, lives with those possessions they consider essential for survival. Which, if you think about it, is the core of minimalism. Living with what is essential to life and discarding what is not necessary.

Human beings are meant to find a sense of security and a meaning in life through relationships, both with people and the environment. Material possessions are incidental to that purpose. And this is what minimalism is, that is, living with the essentials that you value and make you happy.

3. *Living a life that is full.* A full life does not mean having more and doing more. What full life means are doing the things you love to do, having time with the people you love, being passionate about things, ideas, activities that matter, and enjoying what you do each moment. This description of a full life does not require an excess of material possessions or that you overwork yourself. Minimalism calls for you to focus the attention and intentions on the essentials.

Simple Guide to Becoming a Minimalist

Contrary to what many believe, minimalism is attainable. At the initial stages, being a minimalist may not be easy. However, you become successful as a minimalist if you stay focused with your goal of living a simple life. Here are simple steps you can do to start you off:

1) *Disengage yourself from present realities.* Take time to detach yourself from reality and take a look at your life. Try to evaluate what you do, your past actions, what makes you happy and content, and your plans for the future.

2) *Make a list of goals.* Make a list of the realities you see. From this list, make another short list that you believe are the most important to you and compare your long list from your short list.

3) *Discard the nonessentials.* The items that you included in the short list are the essentials. The items that are not on your short list are the nonessentials that you need to throw away. Throwing away the nonessentials could be difficult, and choosing could be emotional. But, choosing the essentials is necessary, if you are intent on living a simple life.

4) *Transition to a minimalist life*style does not happen overnight. Therefore, be patient and transition gradually into a minimalist way of life. For instance, you are passionate about painting because you need to work hard to pay the bills. You can indulge a little of your time on your passion, while you work

full-time to pay the bills. Start your transformation with small changes. When you get familiar with your new life, you can then move on to bigger challenges.

Many people view minimalism with skepticism. The demands of minimalism make it difficult for one with a materialistic outlook to give up all the possessions acquired through the years. Not understanding the essence of minimalism, what it is trying to correct, and its aims make people's outlook on minimalism unattainable.

But for one who aspire for a positive change in life, minimalism is achievable and sustainable. One needs to realize and accept that sacrifice is needed for change. But, what you sacrifice is worth what you achieve to live a life that is free of stress.

Chapter 2: Minimalism and the Search for Happiness

In this Chapter, I am going to tell you about the relationship of minimalism to what people aspire to, that is, happiness. The chapter provides answers to the following questions:

- What is happiness and why is it elusive?
- What are the benefits you get from minimalism?
- What are the stages one goes through to become a minimalist?
- How does minimalism manifest in day-to-day living?
- How can a minimalist reconcile the appearance of multiple acts of minimalism?

There is, perhaps, no one who does not aim for happiness as the end-goal in this life. Everything that people do from day-to-day is but a means to achieve happiness. But, achieving happiness is problematic and elusive.

Contrary to what many believe, happiness is a state of the mind. Happiness is not just possessing material things. However, there are many who base their happiness in the material things they own. As a result of this belief, there is the obsession to accumulate things. To acquire more material things, you work hard to earn more. In the process of working hard, you sacrifice relationships with people who matter to you. And, after all the hard work and the possessions, happiness is still elusive.

The source of happiness is not from the external things and people around you. Happiness comes from within you. This state of mind comes to you out of your experiences with the outside world. The emotions you feel, and the intellectual content drawn from the experience dictate your state of mind.

Minimalism could be the means to free you from obsessions, negative thoughts and emotions. When you are free from what drags you down, you can enjoy the following advantages:

- Change your negative thoughts to positive ones
- Be in control of your time and space, which you can use instead to strengthen your relationship with loved ones or with people who are important to you
- Focus on your health
- Pursue activities that you are passionate about
- Grow with meaningful life experiences
- Contribute to others
- Live without excess

The Process of transformation to a minimalist life

Deciding to live a minimalist life is one thing, and going through the process of transformation is another. You may go through a tough psychological development in becoming a minimalist.

Crisis. The process starts with the realization that a problem exists in your life. The problem could be anything, like feeling crowded with things, people, or ideas which make you feel a need for space to breath or clear your head. The crisis could come from medical concerns, work, or domestic issues. There is a nagging feeling that things should change and you realize that if things remain as they are, you lose more in life.

Curiosity. You hear of the concept of minimalism, and you know it is a trending phenomenon. You get interested, but you don't know much of minimalism. The point is, it is curiosity which drives you to search for answers to your problem. Believing you found the solution, you decide to give minimalism a try.

Apprehension. Minimalism is new to you. And as in every change, it is the jump that is scary. So, you hesitate, and you begin to doubt your decision. Minimalism is about letting go of things, of the past that holds you back, of ideas that exist to clutter your mind, and activities you have the habit of doing. The apprehension is understandable, but you could remind yourself of your decision to change your life and stay focused on your goal.

Release. Letting go is like cutting the umbilical cord, a separation that could be painful. Getting rid of the familiarities like the things you own, ideas, beliefs or people are difficult. You can make 'letting to' easy through a gradual change. Start with a small change like throwing away stuff that is easy to for you to deal with: old clothes, books that stayed on the shelf for years or old furniture. When you succeed at this stage, move on to removing more sentimental pieces.

Disappointment. The time will come when you miss what you have thrown away; then you begin to doubt your decision. They were once a part of your life and your activities. Regret creeps in and remorse. Accept the feeling and move on. You have gone through the reasons why you need to throw them away. Stick to your decision with determination.

Gratitude. Once you are over the disappointment stage, you feel relieved. You succeeded in getting over the emotional struggle of separation from things, ideas, and people. Now that you are free of the inessentials, you can enjoy the space and focus on the essentials. You will be grateful that you now have the opportunity to give attention to what you neglected in your obsession to work hard: strengthen your ties with people, focus on productive ideas, and have time for your passion.

Empowerment. Minimalism gives you the freedom from all your obsessions. What is more significant is that you control your life. It gives you the confidence to chart your path and be in control. You still can own possessions, but the choice is yours and not because of an outside influence.

Wholistic. As mentioned, a beginner minimalist can start with any problem, like decluttering the home space. Decluttering of a physical space is the beginning, but you will find that decluttering could apply to other areas of your life as well, like in a work environment when you declutter ideas and work relationships, relationships with other people, and activities. The idea of minimalism is to remove the nonessentials so you can focus and improve on what matters to you most.

The Many Faces of Minimalism

Needs motivate a person's behavior, which varies depending on the kind of need that dominates at a particular time. Borrowing from the categories made by Allport and Maslow, there are eight categories: physiological needs (food, shelter, and clothing), safety needs, social needs (love and belonging), esteem (such as status, recognition, self-esteem), and self-actualization. Other experts divide self-actualization into cognitive needs (thirst for knowledge and meaning), aesthetic needs (that is, the appreciation of beauty and harmony), and self-actualization (the realization of a person's potentials, self-fulfillment, and peak experiences)

Further, these needs can show in your ideas, in the choice of relationships, the activities you engage in, and in your thoughts. Minimalism, therefore, penetrates all of human thoughts, emotions, behavior, and each act of minimalism adds a value to your life. The list given below are not inclusive, and you may find a couple more as you make minimalism a way of life.

- *Possessions minimalist* – This kind of minimalist gets rid of material possessions to allow for more physical space. Decluttering possessions enable you to breathe, removes the feeling of being crowded, and helps clear thoughts.
- *Thought minimalist* – A minimalist who throws away ideas that do not add value to life. Removing negative thoughts and ideas allow you to focus on constructive ideas and positive thoughts that matter. It might amaze you to discover that inculcating positive ideas and thoughts can make you a positive person.
- *Money minimalist* – The popular belief is that having more money gets you more possessions, thereby, improving your social and economic status. The money

minimalist tells you to get along in life with what you have.

- *Decision minimalist* – With ideas limited to what adds value to your life, you make fewer decisions. Fewer decisions to make each day translates to less stress.
- *Distraction minimalist* – This minimalist reduces distractions from the environment and creates a conducive environment. A conducive environment enables you to focus on neglected passion and operate less based on willpower.
- *Interpersonal conflict minimalist* – A minimalist who takes time to know and understand other people. In getting to know the other people better, you get to respect their individuality and they respect yours. The knowledge you gain about other people can improve and strengthen your relationship.
- *Difficulty minimalist* – where you analyze the steps you need to do to get things done. You break the process down into manageable steps, disregard steps that are not important, and retain those that are necessary. You save time and effort in paring down the steps.
- *Commitment minimalist* – where you make promises you are sure you can commit to without doing harm to

others. By doing so, you reduce the interpersonal conflict and motivational friction.

- *Moment minimalist* – Where you maximize the time you spend on things and people you consider important. Doing the moment minimalist reduces or eliminates your wasted moments that lead to regrets and frustrations. The moment minimalist maximizes quality time with people who matter.
- *Expectation minimalist* – Having expectations from people and things often lead to disappointments. By removing or reducing your expectations and by being open to new experiences, you intentionally eliminate the stress from your life.

The kinds of minimalism mentioned above are not independent of each other. Each kind of minimalism can happen simultaneously, or one can happen as a consequence of another act. An example is when you buy a used car to save money. Contrary to what you believe, buying a used car will cost more in terms of time, money for the maintenance, and the trouble you experience in the process.

In mixing several kinds of minimalism, you need to decide on priorities and make tradeoffs. Without prioritizing, you will get frustrated and fall into the trap of negative thoughts and feelings.

What you can do in moments where you feel like backsliding is to maximize the goal of minimalism, which is to simplify your life, set priorities, and focus on what matters most to you.

Chapter 3: Minimalism as Counter Consumerism

In this chapter, I am going to tell you how minimalism can counter the culture of consumerism that is dominating today's society. The chapter provides answers to the following questions:

- What are the effects of consumerism?
- What is the larger psychological impact of consumerism on people?
- What are the responses of minimalism?
- What can you do to counter consumerism?
- What benefits do you get when you resist the culture of consumerism?

To associate minimalism with consumerism is understandable. Studies of human needs shifted its focus from identifying the basic needs (that is, food, shelter, and clothing) to investigating how people define their needs and transform these interpretations into decisions and actions. An observed increase in consumerism in the last few decades may have triggered the shift in the study of human needs. Further, a shift in consumer preference from mass produced brands to personalized products and services was also evident.

Minimalism became popular with the phrase "Less is More", which, in turn translates into economic consumption. However, Minimalism is broader than material consumption and encompass ideas, thoughts, relationships, aesthetics, and activities. In fact, minimalism as a way of life covers all aspects of human behavior. To limit the understanding of minimalism into economic consumption is misleading.

Effects of consumerism and the response of minimalism

Consumerism is not just a name to categorize a particular human behavior; consumerism evolved with the realities of the time. There was a significant increase in income and wealth in the last 20 years. Business and industry latched on to this phenomenon by producing goods laterally and vertically, making products accessible to a wider market. Add the influence of media and advertising and you have an increase in buying consumption.

You might think that making products and services available to a wider market is good for the consumers, there are effects that would eventually give rise to minimalism as a response.

Effects of Consumerism

- The growth in the level and share of income and wealth led to luxury spending
- Wider income distribution,
- Women entering the corporate world,

- The growing importance of the digital world
- The appearance of the concept of "rising expectations" or aspirations of people

You might say that there is nothing wrong with the effects of consumerism where 'more means more' to people. But, there are larger psychological impact on the consumers that calls for critical attention:

- *Materialist values.* There are a lot of studies to show that the materialist values have a negative impact on a person's well-being.
- *Work stress.* With the increased income, people's aspirations soar. People must work long hours to be able to spend more. Working long hours reduce your time spent with people, destroying relationships and cutting you off from the social connections and community involvement. As consumption competition escalates, you endanger your sources of well-being : friendship, family, peers, and community.
- *The destruction of the environment.* Excessive consumption adversely affects the environment in a big way. The destruction of the environment, in turn, adversely affects the quality of life of the people.

What you can do to counter consumerism

The urge to buy comes from fears and insecurities. The business world capitalizes on people's fears and insecurities and uses media advertising to create the compulsion to buy more. Because of this compulsion, you fall into the trap of "work more to spend more." You need to stop the cycle of working and spending and distinguish between wants and needs.

You can follow the suggestions below and come out in control of your situation:

1) *Be aware of your impulses.* Being aware of your body directs your attention to the impulses.

2) *Pause and evaluate your intended action.* Ask yourself questions, like: Do you need the item you are about to buy? Will the item add value to your life? Pausing also gives you time for the urge to fade. Or you can force yourself to wait, say for a week or a month. Perhaps, in a week or a month's time, the urge disappears.

3) *Stop emulating other people.* Each person is unique and you have your needs specific to your lifestyle. You also do not have to follow a trend. The current fashion may not suit your personality and you regret buying an item not suitable nor appropriate for your person.

4) *Know yourself and identify your weaknesses.* It is easy to get into a habit and quite difficult to get out of it. A habit could

become trigger points for your weaknesses, like a favorite product, a store, an addiction, and attractive price promotions. You win the battle halfway in recognizing your weaknesses and identifying trigger points.

5) *Check your motivations.* Good advertising lures you into buying a product with promises that cater to your imagined needs. These promises need not have facts to support the claims. Check your motives for buying the product: Are you buying the product because a friend happens to own one (envy)? Are you buying the product so people would know you are hip and trendy (the need to belong)? Be objective and honest in answering these questions.

6) *Choose a product that adds value to you or to others.* Buying a product that is useful to others answers a higher human need of self-fulfilment and self-actualization.

7) *Check for hidden costs in the product.* Buying a product involves more than the cost. For instance, buying a cheap car may have saved you money. But, in choosing a cheap car, you sacrifice your time in maintenance and travel, cost you more for constant repairs, and hassle. The initial happiness you get in acquiring the car soon fades with the stress and worry it brings you later.

8) *Test your limits.* If you are a compulsive buyer in the past, this step may prove difficult. But, this is a challenge as to how far you can go with your goal of living a life that is simple. Force yourself to refrain from shopping for a month or two. Extend the time limit as you go along with this experiment. Your success is its own motivation until you reach the point of making rule of limiting shopping to the essentials a way of life.

Gains when minimalism counters consumerism

1. *A reduced debt.* On the plus side, using a credit card is convenient for the consumer. Credit cards make daily purchases easy. And, with online buying, you get what you want without leaving the house. However, the use of credit card is also the easiest way to incur debt, and the fastest way to accumulate debt. As the pressure mounts for you to pay the debts, you feel the need to work more hours to increase your income. The accumulated debt and the pressure to work more lead to stress in your life.

2. *Reduced desire for possessions.* The possessions you accumulated for years require your time and energy in maintenance and order. The tasks you do like maintaining property, replacing furniture or equipment, fixing a vehicle, cleaning ornaments, organizing

accessories on your desk could drain you physically and emotionally.

3. *Decreased desire for upscale lifestyle norms.* Before, envy extends to the regular John living next door. The media and advertising channels, which painted the life of the rich and famous as glamorous and superior brought envy on their lifestyle. And, because the lifestyle norm of the rich is beyond the income of ordinary people, the result is stress. The only way to stop the envy is through intentional rejection.

4. *Reduction of adverse impact on the environment.* The earth has enough resources to supply people's needs. The resources, however, become depleted when people try to satisfy their wants. Exhausting earth's resources to satisfy people's wants, which are unnecessary, is disastrous for mankind.

5. *Less need to follow the trend.* Keeping up with the latest trends gives one the feeling of belonging, of being in a group, and of being one with the time. Not to be in with the trend means being left behind. Consumerism, on the other hand, needs consumers to keep on spending on their products. So products expand and fashion change

shortly after its introduction. Consumerism ties you to its culture, opting out frees you from its bondage.

6. *Less pressure to impress others with material possessions.* Conspicuous consumption is a phrase used by Thorstein Veblen in 1899, an economist, to describe a specific class. The phrase refers to consumers who buy expensive materials as status symbols which hide the real needs of the buyers. Conspicuous consumption uses the image of wealth to promote the self, hiding the reality of the consumer. Image building through conspicuous consumption is still true today and is causing stress for many.

7. *More generosity.* When you opt out of consumerism, you free your energy, time, and resources to focus on what matters most to you. You also discover that giving to others, whether it is your time and resources, is more satisfying than spending on unnecessary things. By creating space within you, generosity can fill part of that space in your life.

8. *More Contentment.* Many people search for contentment, believing that desire for consumption follows. This belief, however, is a misconception. Contentment comes with the intentional rejection of consumerism.

Minimalism realigns your life with your passion, finding joy and contentment in doing so.

9. *Greater ability to see through empty claims.* When you are free from biases and negative influences, you can distinguish between the authentic claims from the inauthentic ones. Seeing reality with clarity helps you make decisions out of informed choices.

10. *Greater realization that this world is not just material.* Intentional rejection of consumerism makes you realize that happiness does not come from material things but from what is not seen, such as love, faith, hope, and the aesthetics.

As mentioned, minimalism does not limit its scope to economic consumption. Minimalism penetrates all aspects of human behavior and attempts to correct those behaviors that do not add value to life. In our present society where the culture of consumerism is dominant and impacts people adversely, a discussion on consumerism and how to counter this culture becomes imperative.

The Message of Minimalism

When most picture the idea of being a minimalist, they may imagine a house filled with very few modernized objects and the color white in every room. Yes, this could be a pretty accurate picture of those that are extreme minimalists or those that do not enjoy being surrounded by modern technology. However, that is not what this book is about. Many people see it as a fad, rather than a way of life that they could just as easily incorporate into their everyday lifestyles. The point of minimalism is not to live with less than 100 items, to get rid of your flat screen television or vehicle, or to travel the world with just a backpack and a heart full of adventure. But minimalism can help you accomplish all those things, if you wish to!

In reality, minimalism is just a tool that people utilize to simplify their lives. It is a way to reach and truly achieve a point of freedom in their conventional life. Think about what it would be like to have fewer material belongings to sift through on a daily basis? Think about what it would be like to step beyond the box of the consumer culture we all have fallen into? The key aspects of minimalism can help!

Now, there is absolutely nothing wrong with owning material things. But we humans nowadays have given too much meaning and credit behind the things we own. You must be rich and well off if you own an expensive automobile. You must be a healthy individual if you own a treadmill. You must be a fashionista if you own many articles of clothing. The items that we surround ourselves with have given other human beings around us permission to assume what our lives are like, who we are as people and how we conduct ourselves. This is the box of consumerism we have allowed ourselves to become encased in. And it is time to put these ideas to rest. And where better to start but within your own life?

Minimalism also allows us to make crucial decisions about our life much easier and simpler. The ways of minimalism push us to strive for better, instead of allowing ourselves to become overly obsessed with material possessions in various ways. I know what you are thinking, "How in the world can I become a minimalist or incorporate that lifestyle into MY life? It sounds terrible." Again, this is the image that society has put into our minds! Minimalism is a tool that allows one to get rid of the excesses of life by focusing on what is more important, so you can seek and achieve freedom, fulfillment and pure, blissful happiness.

Minimalism assists us by:

- Discovering our real purpose and mission in this lifetime
- Getting rid of the superfluous items we don't need or use
- Contributing to our communities
- Maturing as individual people
- Focusing on our health, creating a better temple to reside in
- Allowing room for creativity
- Experiencing the idea of REAL freedom
- Pursue things that we are passionate about

- Save our time for things that matter more
- Eliminate our feelings of discontent

As human beings, we naturally want to be happy and are constantly searching for **things** instead of life experiences or other people to fulfill this empty feeling that resides inside of many of us. Much of the population has a false sense of what is necessary to survive and thrive today, and it is about pinpointing what makes our lives the most superfluous. We all unknowingly live, surrounded by things that actually make us more miserable. And it is time you put a stop to this in your own life and make a change. It is time to make the best **better**.

The following chapters will introduce you to ways to incorporate minimalism into your life. No need to go out and buy a gallon of white paint – we are not extremists here. You **will** have to put in some work, as well as work through temptations. But this book is here to help you make your life simpler, so you can live life happier!

The Process of Simplifying your Life

You are here for one reason: to simplify your life. You want to feel better about your time here on Earth, but you cannot do so without making some changes first. Adding a nice dose of simplicity into your everyday lifestyle will bring you joy, ultimate freedom, and a nice balance to reside in.

"Purity and simplicity are the two wings with which man soars above the earth and all temporary nature" – Thomas Kempis.

This chapter is full of important aspects that your life constantly revolves around that you can simplify with some time, dedication and a vow to yourself. What is not to like about the sound of living in a more freeing world that you have created yourself? Yeah, that's what I thought. Here are some vital aspects you can start simplifying piece by piece right away!

Multitasking – We conduct the act of multitasking in an effort to get more done at a faster rate, so we can accomplish more throughout the day. Great thinking, but did you know you are actually causing yourself to be more stressed? Handling ONE task at a time, in the long run, can assist you in accomplishing more because you have your full attention on whatever you are in the process of completing! You are also more proud and feel more fulfilled by things you do well.

Disconnect – We are not saying to throw away all your mobile devices, but it is vital to learn when to disconnect from the world for a bit. Learn to reprioritize, and you will be bombarded by fewer distractions, which will result in accomplishing many more tasks that make us feel better at the end of the day.

Artificial ingredients – This one may sound a bit weird, but it makes total sense. Avoiding the bad things that we fuel our bodies with majorly assists in becoming a better minimalist. We consume loads of refined grains, sodium and sugars on a constant basis. Reducing the consumption of these things that are initially bad for our bodies, which we should treat more like temples, will be much better for you in the long term. This includes over the counter medications as well. This, in itself, will help you unpack your medicine cabinet.

Debt – There are millions of people that are trapped by their debt. Start the process of reducing it, today. Even if it a small amount here and there, that is progress! Do not become weighted down by purchasing things you do not need. Don't let objects determine your happiness or worth. Sacrificing luxurious things today can lead you to a path of a debt free future.

Negativity – As many of us know, always having your mind boggled with negative thoughts and emotions can greatly wave our decisions, especially our purchasing decisions. Having hate, regret or resentment towards others has never gotten anyone very far. Your mind and the way you utilize it is YOUR responsibility. Replace negative feelings with positive ones! Do something for someone else occasionally. A great way to feel better about yourself is to make someone else feel good!

Goals – It is time to prioritize. Instead of having many goals that you have intentions to half achieve, choose ones that mean more to you, and make efforts to strive for those most important to you. This will also greatly improve your rate for succeeding at accomplishing your goals!

Time commitments – The majority of us live in a constant state of hurry, living out hectic lifestyles with no light at the end of the tunnel. Which can be extremely exhausting! It is crucial to be able to take some time to yourself, to do things for yourself, whether that is being active in a hobby that interests you, etc. Release yourself from the commitments that do not mean as much to the value of your life. Most importantly, make commitments to yourself.

Possessions – You probably wondered when we would hit the subject of material things, huh? It is no secret that having too many things can clutter not only our physical surroundings, but they can tend to clutter our mind as well. Think about how many hours you put in a day moving things around, cleaning them and maintaining them? A LOT. This takes us away from things that are more important, namely experiencing things or helping others that need a hand, to name a couple. Inanimate objects drain our energy, our wallets, and our attention spans. It is time to invest time in yourself and your loved ones, instead of in the things that surround and plague you!

How to Get the Most out of Life's Experiences

A big part of living the minimalistic lifestyle is learning how to engulf yourself into the smallest of moments that life has to offer. It is about teaching yourself to get the most out of everything you have the opportunity to experience! This chapter is full of unique ways that not many have pondered over. These are ways to take back YOUR life and live it to the fullest extent.

Embrace creativity – Despite popular belief, the greatest of minds are not fueled by book smarts, but by creativity. If you haven't found your muse, dive into different activities, even ones outside your comfort zone. You will find what fuels that imagination of yours in no time!

Rules can be broken – Now, this is not permission to go out and start breaking the law. The law is there for a reason. But, there are plenty of other rules that are meant to be pushed and possibly broken. If we obeyed them all, humanity would not be where it is at this very moment. If you are curious, find ways to feed that curiosity. Ask questions, be imaginative. Break those rules, make new ones, and then find ways to break them as well. Without rule breakers, there would be NO progress in the world. You would not have a smartphone, but rather a bag phone more than likely.

You are not inferior – If you have people that make you feel like less of a person, put a stop to it. Stop that way of thinking. No one is better than you, has a better brain than you, etc. People do not reach their goals or achieve any kind of ambitions with this mindset! The most well-known people have been rejected a time or two in their lifetime – in fact, they've definitely been rejected more! "Success is never permanent, and failure is never fatal." – John Wooden. Remember that!

Slow down and bask – Our hectic schedules cause many of us to be constantly in a rush, ALL the time, even when we are not constrained by time limits. Patience is quite the virtue to have, these days. Ensure that you are giving yourself time to function. Leave for work or timely destinations early, so that you can drive at your leisure and take in the scenery. When walking your dog, allow your pet to explore and take in the sights and sounds of the world around it. Just the simplicity of taking your time is a break within itself. Take a breath. Both your mental and physical health will thank you graciously.

Upset? Act. – We are all guilty of complaining about some aspect of our lives at some point of another. Facebooking our opinions will do nothing to change the world. If you are truly upset with something, do something about it! Write a blog, create a video to share with your friends on your social media. Kindly protest. If you have no intentions to stand up, do not complain. I always keep in mind one of Gandhi's better-known quotes: "Be the change you wish to see in the world."

Think less, do more – You should research and educate yourself before diving into important decisions in life. If not, you can get yourself into a mess of trouble, or even debt. But that is not an excuse to leave your life in a state of limbo over a decision. You will paralyze yourself, and will only become more stuck as time passes on. Gather what you need to know, and proceed. Take a risk if you must!

You are never alone – Two heads (or several) are better than one! One pair of hands can do amazing things, but when you put a team of brilliant minds together, many things are possible! No one has ALL the answers, but you can answer your questions if you collaborate with other individuals. Surround yourself with positive people who can assist you in further development.

Take a closer look – Many people do not know how, or ever take the time to, but it is important to step into the shoes of another person from time to time. This can help you and another person come to a new perspective and avoid arguments that are just a waste of time.

Ways to De-Clutter your Life

We literally spend **years** collecting pointless items that we work to keep track of and maintain. Material things do not equal happiness, and never can. In reality, all inanimate objects are distractions to some extent or another. Did you know that there are more storage facilities in America than there are McDonald's restaurants combined worldwide? This chapter will go over ways to start the de-cluttering process of your life.

Decision time – Before you begin to chuck stuff into boxes, write down the reasons as to WHY you wish to de-clutter your life from material possessions. Saving money? Gaining space? Less stress? No matter the reason, looking at that list will keep you motivated and on the right path!

Reclaim time – One of the best parts of minimalism is the ability to crank back that clock and reclaim some of your wasted time that you spend shopping for more stuff, rearranging to make room, storing, repairing or maintaining it!

Valuables – One of the tougher parts of ridding yourself of stuff is choosing things that truly **matter** to you. Decide on the things that hold the most value to you, and rid yourself of the rest.

Reduce – There are certain things you cannot throw away, but you can reduce! You do not need ten sets of sheets for one person, or hundreds of dishes for a family of four- this only creates more work for you.

Wardrobe – Known as Project 333, the concept is simple. Choose 33 items of clothing that you wish to see over 3 months time, and donate or store the rest. You will be amazed at how many items you don't need or wear. You will no longer be stressed about what to wear because all of your clothing will be your favorite pieces.

Charity box – Find some boxes and fill them up with items that you no longer have a use for, or that you do not value as much. Donate to charity or thrift stores. The environment will thank you, but so will those that are less fortunate.

Sentimental evaluation – The hardest items for people to let go are those that hold some type of sentimental value, obviously. Decide which things you want to keep, and which things that you could toss, such as old birthday cards or ticket stubs. Again, minimalism is not about getting rid of all of your things, but finding meaning in your possessions and tossing what you no longer have a need for.

Simplify your routine – We could all use a bit of sprucing up when it comes to cutting down our routines, especially our morning ones! This comes after the steps of de-cluttering your bathroom accessories, as well as making breakfast in a slimmed-down kitchen. Having less to worry about helps you start out your days in a much better mood!

Car clean-out – We all should be doing this, but when our backseats are hardly occupied by people, we take advantage of all that room. Get rid of the extra clothes, food wrappers etc. A clean car is about as important as a clean home!

Time to digitize – While a certain amount of technology can also pile up our lives, imagine a home office without all those stacks of papers to sort through? Take a weekend to scan important documents and put them on a flash drive or another safe place. This also means old photographs as well.

Embrace the new, minimize old media – Canceling newspaper and magazine subscriptions will not only save you money, but they are one less thing to throw away and/or dust around. This goes for the number of things we soak in new media on too. We really only need one television, one phone, etc.

Borrow instead of purchasing – If you need an item that you know you are only going to utilize once, ask around to see if a family member or friend has it, or check the local thrift store. This goes for things for parties, books, etc.

Buy experiences, not objects – Instead of window browsing at the mall and then buying yet another pair of shoes, try putting your hard-earned money into an experience instead, such as a cooking demo, book weekend, wine tasting, outdoor activities, etc. The experience will last MUCH longer that a pair of heels!

Quality versus quantity – If you do have to purchase an item, it is better to go for those that are going to last you awhile, so you do not have to go out and continuously buy the same item. Your bank account will embrace you with a hug for this! Whenever I'm planning on purchasing an item, I make sure to find at least two purposes it will serve me.

Get rid of 1 thing a day – It is important to start small when minimizing things in your home. For many, the "rid 1 per day" rule works wonders! Make a promise to yourself to get rid of at least one item (or more!) each and every day. It is a slow process, but you will see progress!

Chapter 4: Letting Go and Moving On

In this chapter, I am going to tell you about letting go of the past so you can move on to a new stress-free life. The chapter aims to answer the following questions:

- What does letting go mean?
- Is 'letting go' limited to throwing away material possessions?
- How do you let go of stressful habits?
- How do you let go of negative thoughts, emotions, and beliefs?
- What do I gain from letting go of the past?

People are products of their past life experiences from childhood to their adult life. Parents tell their children to be more, to achieve high, to accumulate degrees, to possess things, have more friends, marry and have children, to earn more money. Business and media seduce people into buying products. What becomes embedded in the minds of people is the message that a happy life comes from having more of everything.

What is lacking in the path to happiness above is the letting go of the past, of friends and other people, of attitude, emotions, beliefs, and practices which are the hidden key to achieving a full and happy life.

This hidden key leads to your healing and is necessary to make a space for a wonderful life ahead of you.

What Letting Go Means

Letting go could have different definitions and interpretations to different people. The reason for the difficulty differs with each person's fears and insecurities.

Getting Out of Your Comfort Zone. Familiar friends, ideas, and habits make you comfortable and safe. To leave your comfort zone is a threat and, therefore, stressful. A person faced with a problem would make excuses to avoid change. Leaving one's comfort zone often is the primary hurdle one faces when letting go of anything or anybody.

You find difficulty in letting go of a variety of incidents; from the simplest inconvenience to the most tragic incident. The problem could be just getting rid of old clothing or a painful breakup of a long-standing friendship. Whether the separation is simple or tragic, the experience of pain is present. Pain comes in many form, but in whatever form, experiencing pain is normal to a person. It is how you cope with pain that determines your path. There are people who would embrace the pain and move forward, and others who would turn away and remain in their comfort zones.

Letting Go is Accepting the Uncertainties. One cannot tell what lies in the future. Not knowing what to expect when you let go is scary. To stay with the familiar is better than to step into the unknown. In familiar surroundings, you know what you are dealing with, what to expect, and what to do. Which is the exact opposite of the unknown future. It is the uncertainty of the unknown that is the second hurdle one faces in letting go of the past.

The third hurdle is the unpredictability of the future. You might decide to embrace the uncertainty of the future and believe you can prepare for what would happen once there. But, the future is unpredictable due to the interplay of many factors. You never know what happens next, in spite of a well-laid out plan. And this unpredictability is what scares most people, enough to discourage them from moving out of the comfort zone.

The fourth hurdle one has to face when letting go is the absence of reference points in the past to help you in your future journey. The future is new and exploratory, the past is full of reference points to help you evaluate the situation and act. The thought of having nothing to fall back on is alarming. For one not used to making decisions, it could be a scary situation. What is seen that exploring the future and making decisions alone makes a person stronger and firmer in convictions.

The fifth hurdle a person letting go experiences is the belief that in letting go of things, ideas, habits, and people a part of the self, of the identity or personality is left behind. But, what really happens when you let go is make room for the positive in everything.

Letting Go is Forgiving. Forgiving is tough, especially when the pain runs deep. This is the reason why some people refuse to forgive and let go. It is possible for a person to let go and not forgive, but the letting go will not be as clean and pure as when a person forgives and let go. Letting go without forgiving will also make it hard for one to move on.

Forgiving means an absolution; it means letting go of the hatred, of blaming, resentment, anger toward someone or something. Forgiveness is both an attitude and a process. One who has a forgiving attitude does not hold grudges nor judge another person's act or behavior outright. As a process, goes through a stage which could be painful, but ultimately gives you the freedom you need to move on. By forgiving, you create a space within you for the positive things in life.

Letting Go is Separating from Dysfunctional Habits. There are lifestyle habits that are dysfunctional and cause you stress in life.

Examples of dysfunctional living habits are staying out late nights, sleeping late, taking on too many workloads, never saying no to friends' requests, procrastination, and allowing distractions in your life.

Habits are difficult to let go as the regularity of the behavior has become a second skin of a person. The habit is involuntary, therefore, done without so much thought or intention. Breaking a dysfunctional habit is difficult but achievable if you do the following:

- Commit to yourself. Believe in your worth as a person and that, therefore, you deserve a better life. Dysfunctional living habits can change by substituting good habits. One method of breaking a habit is to identify the trigger point and avoid it once identified. For instance, the tendency to watch television after dinner. If the trigger point is the comfortable sofa in front of the television, you could go out of the house for fresh air.
- Avoid extra obligations. The inability to say no to requests from friends and coworkers burden you with an extra load of work. This extra obligations robs you of quality time you could spend for yourself and with your family members. Learn to say no gently, but firmly. Have

that extra time instead for you to do activities you are passionate about. Spend time and bond with family members and friends; this quality time will strengthen your relationship.

- Change a habit, not out of need, but in celebration. When you view change as a celebration for letting go of a habit, the change becomes easy and acceptable. You do not feel forced to change because you need to. A trick you can do to celebrate habit change is to visualize the change in your mind. The vision will help you actualize your resolve to change. Another way of making it easy for you to change a habit is to treat yourself with activities you like, join groups that support habit change, go into therapy like reflexology or yoga.

Letting Go is Ridding Yourself of Negative Emotions, Thoughts, and Beliefs. A lifetime of expectations from parents, friends, and employers to 'be more' lead to fear, resentments, guilt, remorse, and judgements based on unfounded beliefs. These negative emotions and beliefs drag you and keep you from moving forward. However, since these emotions and beliefs are mostly acquired, it lies within you to change.

- Learn and develop self-affirmations. Doing positive affirmations will counter the negative criticisms you received from the past. Receiving constant negative criticisms and judgements affect your self-worth and confidence. Positive self-affirmations will slowly replace the negative emotions and make you realize of your worth as a person.

An example of self-affirmations is "I choose not to be afraid", "I choose to be happy today", "I choose joy rather than sadness", "I ignore useless criticisms."

Know, however, that negative emotions will not go away and stay away. These emotions will recur from time to time. A strong person will accept the negative emotion but will not allow it to stay and take a hold of him again. A changed you will be able to distinguish which emotion adds value to your life and which destroys you.

- Think only of happy thoughts. Learn to say no to the negative thoughts and entertain positive thoughts. If the people around you talk of fears, anger, and insecurities you either step away from the conversation or tell them gently you prefer to talk about what is positive.

If a positive thought is not possible to replace a negative thought, doubting the negative helps. An example is when you have a negative thought, you turn it around with the thought that you could be wrong, and that there is a reason behind the wrong that you do not know anything about.

- Stay tuned to the present. Let old beliefs stay in the past. The present realities are different from the past. Your reality today is different from your past realities. Stay in the present and keep focused on the 'here and now'. You can make your self-affirmation saying "I choose now" and that you are okay when and where you are. These self-affirmations will help counter negative beliefs and attitudes that got embedded from the past.
- Avoid comparing yourself with others. No two persons are the same in attributes and essence; each one is unique. To compare yourself with others is a useless exercise. There will always be one who is stronger or weaker than you are, one who is happier, masterful, successful.

You could try living your life your way and set an example for others to emulate. Be a friend, a partner or a colleague rather than a competitor. Stay away from people who makes comparisons and confuse you in the process. You do not need them if you know who you are and what makes you different from others.

- Refrain from 'going against' for the sake of argument. Rebelling appears to be popular nowadays, and attractive, especially to the youth. Rebelling is a waste of time and keeps you from moving on. If you feel you are rebelling, take a pause and reflect on the situation: what triggered the feeling of rebellion?, Will this add value to your life? Will you be able to move on from here?

- Be generous. This value is often overlooked both in its significance as an act and as an importance to you and others. The act of generosity elicits a feeling of satisfaction and fulfillment from the generous person. The feeling that you get from being generous counteracts the negative thoughts, emotions, and beliefs you encountered in the past.

What You Gain From Letting Go of the Past

The past is so embedded in a person that it is difficult and stressful to break away from it. But, perhaps, knowing what you get when you do break off from the past will motivate you to start the process now. Life has so much to offer you that it is a waste to delay this further.

- **You see people without their masks.** It could be an amazing experience to connect with people without their masks. You get to know who and what they are. In connecting with people who are true in the relationship allows you to learn about their perspectives, opinions, and lifestyle. You could learn from these people and grow from the experience. Knowing a person makes you respect them as a person and gives allowances for the uniqueness of each person.

- **You Grow as a Person.** The misunderstanding people have about another person often weighs much on that person. You may have experienced misunderstandings from people about you. As a result of these misunderstandings, you suffered the loss of opportunities, bore the pain of broken relationships, and lost precious friends. A strong person never allows another's misunderstanding of your person to influence and control your life. You know that people will see what they want to see. Entertaining the misunderstanding, therefore, is a futile exercise. Celebrate, instead, your new person.

- **You Gain Internal Peace.** When you succeed in letting go of all the negativity in your surroundings, from whatever source, you gain freedom from external control and influences. People get disturbed and worried by things and events happening to them. What these people do not realize is that it is not the events and situations that bother them, but their attitude and beliefs acquired in the past.

It is not the event or the situation that is bothersome, but how the people view the events. When you let go of fears, worries, negative attitude and beliefs you are able to view the event objectively. The knowledge you get from understanding the event objectively gives you internal peace.

- **You learn more of how life works.** Letting go is not only about breaking away from external negative influences and control. Letting go is also about throwing away your tendency to control and influence others. By wanting to influence and control others, you fail to see the real picture in your effort to create your own reality. But, when you let go and allow things to happen the way they should without your manipulation, you learn more of life and how it works.

People not only accumulate material possessions from the past. Non material possessions also accumulate and become embedded in the personality of the person, blocking the person's ability to move on to a better life. The non materials possessions are your negative thoughts, emotions, and beliefs that dictate how you behave in the present. If the goal is to live a happy and healthy life, then change require letting go of past beliefs and emotions that block your path. Letting go is not easy, but achievable is you stay focused on your vision.

Chapter 5: Minimalism and Financial Freedom

In this chapter, I am going to tell you about how the practice of minimalism has a positive impact on your finances by spending only on the essentials. In this chapter you will find answers to the following questions:

- What is financial freedom?
- What are some truths about financial freedom?
- What stages does one go through to attain financial freedom?
- What are the reasons why many fail to achieve financial freedom?
- Are there personal reasons for failing to achieve financial freedom?

Minimalism's core principle of 'less is more' may convey the message of frugality. Minimalism, however, is much more than spending less and having less of the stuff. While minimalism does preach about "spending less", the root of this phrase is to reduce your financial worries so you can focus on what matter most to you.

In a society where you get seduced by advertisements and media to buy products, you find yourself surrounded by clutter at home and at work. You do not need most of this stuff. Think of what you could have done with the money you spent on the stuff had you given the purchase a mindful thought.

This is what the chapter is about. It tells you how the practice of minimalism can impact your finances and help you spend money on what matters. By limiting your purchase to the essentials, you save money and spend less.

Financial Freedom in Brief

There are people whose purpose in working hard is to earn money, and more money. The idea of having more money is to become rich, believing that being rich makes life convenient. Money becomes the driving force in making personal and professional decisions. Money becomes so all-consuming that it becomes the cause of friction in relationships.

Hopefully, at this point you realize that money is not everything in life. And you start thinking of how you can free yourself from the money trap and be free.

Financial Freedom is not having to worry about money; it is freedom from financial worries. Not having to worry about money means not allowing money to play a dominant role in your life. The key word here is 'not allowing..' Instead of money influencing your behavior, in financial freedom, you take control and not be a slave of money.

Here are some thoughts to go by:

- *Financial freedom is more than being rich.* Confusing the two concepts is easy to understand, especially if one only looks at the surface. For many, being rich makes you free from life's problems. But, rich people have problems, too. Even bigger financial problems. While there are those who earn enough and feel free.
- *There is no limit to spending.* If you have fallen into the trap of consumerism, then spending has become a habit. And for the habitual spender, there is no limit to spending. Whether you are rich or not financially well-off and you spend more than what you need, you are not free from money.
- *Earning more money will not bring you financial freedom.* Earning money is just part of the story, not all of it. There are other ways and elements to attain financial freedom which you need to work on. If you stop at earning money, you will not be financially free. These elements are:
    - An income to sustain you without needing to work. This income is automatic which you get from passive

income, interest savings, and building an emergency fund worth one year of income.

- Spend less than what you earn. The problem most people suffer today is spending more than what they earn. The presence of credit cards make spending easy, not realizing you are spending more than what you earn. Before you know it, you are deep in debt and full of stress.
- Low poverty threshold. Before you raise your brows, poverty threshold here is the minimum amount you need to live a comfortable life. It does not mean going below the poverty line. Low poverty threshold as viewed here is psychological in perspective. It means, you are willing to sacrifice to make bigger and better changes in your life. It makes you reassess your life and distinguish the essentials from the inessentials.

Stages of Financial Freedom

For now, financial freedom is a dream you aspire to get out of the financial situation you are in now. Working towards financial freedom is tough but achievable. It will help you on your journey to financial freedom if you think of what you gain in the end: financial autonomy and self-expression. Financial autonomy and self-expression are values that could bring you towards happiness in life.

First stage – You are solvent enough to meet your financial commitments. In this stage, you no longer rely on outside financial support since you are able to earn more than what you spend. And, you had succeeded in getting out of the debt trap. How long one gets to this stage from dependency is different for each person. It would depend on how hard you work for this goal of solvency.

Second stage – You are financially stable at this stage. At this stage, you have paid all consumer debts, have your emergency savings, and earning income from personal profit. Consumer debts are distinguished from good debts, such as mortgage or educational loans.

Third stage – Here, you can choose how you live and work. Paying your debts and setting aside your savings for emergency purposes has freed you and allowed you to do what you want. You have gone beyond survival point and should you wish, you could quit your job and enjoy life. Money is no longer a dominating force but a tool to build your life. This is a significant aspect of financial freedom - to be free of money's influence and shift your perspective to having meaning in your life.

Fourth stage – This is where you feel secure in the knowledge that your income from investment covers your basic needs. The investment could come from your saving's interest earned and from your passive investments. Security will be an assurance for you, provided you continue with the stages above of spending less than your income.

Fifth stage - You are financially independent at this point. The money you have can sustain your current way of life. Being financially independent, you are freed from worries and can live the way you do as you are when you reach this point.

Sixth Stage – This is where you have enough for your dream lifestyle and some more. You have reached the point where you can enjoy your present lifestyle and makes you free to grow a business, go on a tour and see the world, and pamper yourself with luxuries.

Why Only a Few Succeed in Attaining Financial Freedom

Many dream of financial freedom, yes, and many tried and failed. Knowing why people fail in their attempts will prepare you on your journey towards financial freedom.

- *Delaying* the decision to embark on the journey. Procrastination is a deadly habit, but most people are guilty off this. You keep putting off for tomorrow an act or decision until you find it too late to act on it.
- *Lack of Self – discipline.* The distractions from your environment pulls you everywhere that you have lost focus. You get diverted from your decision to work on financial freedom. It is the lack of discipline that makes you lose your commitment to a goal. You need to

build good daily habits that will help you succeed in your goal. You need goal-building habits to be able to save, invest, and increase your income, for the financial freedom you dream of. Without discipline, it is easy to fall into the trap of procrastination and lose everything.

- *Short-term perspective* – This is the mistake of believing financial freedom is attained on a short term basis. Financial freedom is a process that you have to work on and require sacrifice for bigger changes. Expecting it too soon will lead to frustration.
- *Without perspective* – Most people live day-to-day, spending without thought of its implications, seeing only the gratification of today. Spenders forget that the money spent today when saved could be a tool to live lavishly in the future. This is what minimalist financing is about, delaying gratification for a brighter tomorrow. People also have the mistaken notion that saving is a sacrifice and that they do not need to sacrifice now as they can work for tomorrow. What spenders forget is that saving is knowing what it is you want and accompanying this want with the appropriate action.

Freedom from financial worries is something great to look forward to. It is not only freedom from the money aspect that makes the goal of financial freedom something to work on. Financial freedom gives you the opportunity to live your life to the fullest, the way you intended to.

There are a couple of notes to remember when embarking on your financial freedom. One is that what stops people from working hard on this financial freedom is their personal mental blocks. Removing these mental blocks will open you to developing and having confidence in your skills. The other note is that most of these mental blocks are your own doing. You create your fears which block you from acting. Therefore, since these blocks come from within you, you have the power to change them into positive thoughts and action. You do this and you are on your way to financial freedom.

Chapter 6: Minimalism and Decluttering

In this chapter, I am going to tell you about the positive impact of minimalism on decluttering your space, both on the physical and psychological aspect of an individual. The chapter provides answers to the following questions:

- Is decluttering limited to giving room for physical space?
- What are the underlying reasons why decluttering is difficult to do?
- What are the effects of clutter?
- What do I get from decluttering?
- What guides can I follow in decluttering?

Decluttering is the fad of the day and many are catching on. But, not all truly understand what decluttering is and why declutter. Many believe decluttering is just clearing stuff to have more space to move around. The psychological effects of decluttering is not seen nor recognized.

Another significant aspect missed in the simple interpretation of decluttering is its scope. Decluttering also applies to the clutter in your head, the suffocating presence of unwanted people around you, the flood of information you get from media and social media, and the clutter of ideas in your brain that overwhelm you.

You can also declutter your negative emotions, attitude, habits developed from the past and dragging you down.

Decluttering impacts your life as a whole and when you succeed in decluttering, it might amaze you to see how free you have become to pursue your own purposes and be happy in life.

The underlying reasons for the clutter

You look around your environment and feel dismayed seeing all the clutter that occupies your physical space, at home or in your workplace. Physical clutter is obvious; what lies hidden are the emotional and mental clutter that brings stress to your day-to-day life. So, what makes it difficult to get rid of all the clutter in your life? And what are the reasons the clutter keeps piling up?

Studies on the concept of material acquisitions show that cluttering is a mindset. This mindset makes its appearance in a messy desk, overcrowded shelves, piles of books, and overflowing closets. Since cluttering is a mindset, the source is internal or lie within the individual.

But, what are the underlying reasons for allowing possessions to overfill a space?

1) The trappings of a materialistic world makes material possessions difficult to resist. The works of media and

advertising makes it more difficult to say no to what is new in the market.

2) Emotional attachments to possessions become your emotional baggage. The things a person buys possess memories, symbolizes an individual's dreams. Letting go of these possessions means letting go of those long held memories and forgetting your dreams.

3) Throwing away items could mean an admission of weakness. An admission that the buy was unnecessary or giving away a dress that no longer fits is an admission of defeat in losing weight. It is easy for guilt feelings to follow.

4) And, there is fear. Fear that if we throw away an item, we might regret it later. Fear of feeling guilty for wasting money on an unnecessary item or guilt in knowing you could have used the money on more essential items.

What you gain from decluttering.

1. *Opportunity to have focus on what matters.* With the space created when you removed the clutter, you can concentrate on the tasks on hand. Notice how the clutter around you distracts you from doing what you have to do. You get distracted often and nothing happens. Whether the clutter is in your office or at home, the clutter hinders you from focusing and processing information.

2. *Enhance creativity.* A study done on creativity shows that a clear space helps the creative process. Imagine yourself a writer and you have to work in the middle of several stimuli, like the task of writing, the mess on your desk, and social media. The clutter running simultaneously causes stress and reduces your creativity and productivity.
3. *You get a restful sleep.* Unfinished jobs make for sleepless nights. You worry about deadlines, of needing to do a hundred things and never able to complete one. These unfinished tasks and chores make for your sleepless nights. Without the distraction of the clutter, you are able to finish whatever it is you need to and have a restful sleep. And, a restful sleep benefits your health.
4. *No clutter means positive mood.* Notice how being in the midst of clutter makes you cranky? Clutters are visual noises which can be annoying. A study done in California found that clutter affects mood and self-esteem. This is especially the case for women. The study found a relationship between stress levels and the number of household objects. You can, therefore, view clutter as a signal saying that not all is right with your life.

5. *You let go of your past.* Decluttering has a psychological impact attached on stuff. One reason why a person cannot let go of stuffs are the emotions attached to it. Some stuff reminds you of a significant moment in the past or the stuff was a gift from someone special. You need to evaluate the stuff and the value it has for you now. Or you could start with something less emotional and work on to greater challenges.
6. *You can focus on your goals.* Without the clutter that distracts you, you can concentrate on your goals. The space you created can give you a clear vision of your goals and the opportunity to expand on your goals to ensure its success.

Guide to help you Declutter

1. *Put a stop to the stuff that comes in.* Often, a person declutters only to buy more stuff to replace those that were thrown away. You need strict discipline to commit to decluttering and refrain from buying stuff. You could slow down with your buying, set a schedule (e.g. not buying for a month). When you pass the month without making a purchase, you can extend this until it becomes purposeful, that is, you buy only what you need.
2. *Put away one item a day.* Decluttering need not be hectic. There are advantages in decluttering one item a day.

This tactic makes it easy for you to throw away stuff, especially those that have sentimental value. You won't have to spend much of the day to declutter and do other things instead, from one item it becomes easier to go to harder decisions. If you do this, in time decluttering will be easy.

3. *Have a disposal plan.* Check which from your items you can sell, recycle, or donate. You can have a place or box for each category and place an item into each box every day. When you prepare for decluttering, the task becomes easy.

4. *Decluttering without guilt or obligation.* Decluttering should be a task of celebration and not something you were dictated to by people or other influences. It is a celebration because the space you create after decluttering gives you the freedom to do what you want with the space. Having guilty feelings will only hinder you from your goal and from moving on.

5. *Do not hesitate to let go.* Holding on to things is understandable, but you can avoid this problem by focusing on what you need and not what you want. Things may appear useful to you at the moment, but

upon reflection may show that they do not add value to your life and happiness.

Conclusion

A response results from a crisis felt, and when the response is found effective, it spreads until it becomes a trend. Such is the case of Minimalism. The culture of 'more is more' is the dominant influence of today's society, pulling people towards it. In the age of media and advertisements which present a scripted reality, people cannot help but be pulled towards it. But 'more is more' has its adverse consequences which affect many making life miserable. This condition is what push people to look for relief.

Minimalism as a counter-culture is seen by people as either a movement or a way of life. At the core of minimalism is the belief that 'less is more', the exact opposite of 'more is more.' Not to mistake the meaning of minimalism, 'less' is bigger in scope, touching those that are invisible, such as the positive values of love, hope, beauty, generosity, and faith.

It is not easy making a change from what is familiar to what is new. The change could be painful and even stressful. There will be times when you hesitate and question your decision to live a minimalist life. When you do, look at your present situation and compare that to a life in the future that is free from worries and anxieties. Focus on the vision and stick to your goals.

www.ingramcontent.com/pod-product-compliance
Lightning Source LLC
Chambersburg PA
CBHW071033080526
44587CB00015B/2604